MICHEL ROUX

sauces for meat, poultry & game

Dedication

To my son Alain, who cooks side-by-side with me at The Waterside Inn.

Contents

Foreword

This special category of sauces covers a wide spectrum of ingredients and comes in a vast palette of colours, from yellow ochre to dark mahogany. All are iridescent and lustrous, with the limpidity of water from a mountain spring. Their subtle aromas vary according to their composition and the desired effect. They are all sublime, some, like game sauces, are potent, and all are conducive to conviviality. These sauces are more structured, aromatic and muscular, and have a far longer finish in the mouth than those for fish and shellfish, since they are designed to accompany meat.

The great classic sauces, like Périgueux and Bordelaise Sauce are based on veal stock. They need longer, more complicated preparation, but the effort involved is amply repaid by the enormous pleasure they give your guests, who will appreciate your mastery of the art of sauce-making.

You will be amazed when you discover the sweet, astringent sauces which are my particular favourites. Bigarade Sauce, for example, strikes your tongue like a gentle whiplash. This sauce is perfect served with calves' liver or duck magrets or braised veal tongue.

I have a childhood memory of Maman's ritual Wednesday simmering of a Charcutière Sauce for our lunch. While the sauce was cooking, she would brown some middle-neck pork chops (one of the cheapest cuts you can buy, but also one of the most tender and tasty) in the frying pan. When the chops were cooked to perfection, they exuded a few droplets of juice and were then ready to be coated in the sauce. Perched on a stool, clutching a small knife, I would cut the cornichons into long strips under the watchful and loving eye of my mother. I was so proud when my cornichons were mixed into Maman's sauce! I would rush to be at the table before anyone else, insisting that I had the first serving of the potato purée which she always made with this dish.

Quickly, I made a well in the middle and eagerly held out my plate for her to pour in the sauce. The mélange of purée and sauce sent me into a transport of delight and I could not eat my pork chop until I had been completely engulfed by it (and, of course, begged for a touch more sauce).

Things have changed, however. Nowadays at The Waterside Inn, sauce-making is like a ballet – one dance for my delicate pan-fried poultry, another for my roast Scotch beef and yet another for my Welsh baby lamb en croûte, not forgetting the excellent and abundant game we get from numerous English shoots. Under my conductor's baton, the orchestra of sauce chefs devote their attention to preparing the sauces: purifying, skimming, slowing down or accelerating the cooking, inhaling the aroma and admiring their own reflections in the stockpot before straining the finished product through a muslin cloth or a fine conical sieve. At the climax, they season the sauces to perfection and present each one to me in a tiny pan for my approval. They have danced to my tune and I, the maestro, add the final flourish by carefully pouring the sauce in a ribbon around the meat on the plate just before it leaves the kitchen. And in the dining room the sound of applause is heard as the ballet of sauces comes to its conclusion. What a marvellous aroma, and what a feast for the eyes!

About Stocks

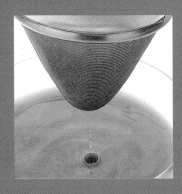

Stocks are the very foundation of sauces: on their quality depends the sucess of your sauces and your mastery of sauce making.

• All the ingredients must be extremely fresh and of the highest quality.

• Equally important – do not drown the stock at the outset by adding too much water to the ingredients; it will make it tasteless and watery. If necessary you can always add more cold water later.

• Always add cold water to a stock. Hot water will make it cloudy and you will lose the desired crystal clarity.

• Cooking a stock for longer does not make it better – quite the reverse. Long cooking can actually be detrimental, since the stock becomes heavy and loses its savour. Follow the cooking times in the recipes precisely.

• For a double depth of flavour, cook the stock twice, using cold water the first time, and the cooled batch of stock the second time.

• In essence, stocks are embryonic sauces, which must be carefully nurtured and titivated. They should be cooked at a simmer and never allowed to boil, and must be skimmed and degreased at regular intervals to remove all impurities. They must be strained gently and delicately through a wire-mesh conical sieve, taking care not to cloud their clarity.

About Sauces

The cook as alchemist

A pinch of this, a pinch of that – the creative process is bewitching. A flame licks up from the pan containing the bubbling, steaming potion, illuminating the sagacious face of the 'saucerer'. He inhales the fumes laden with the first aromas. His imagination is fired as he conjures up the magic of his sauce.

The great sauces

The great classics have been around for centuries. Noble, powerful, aristocratic and elegant, they form part of our heritage. These are sauces fit for feast days and special occasions.

The lesser sauces

There are multitudes of these, suitable for any occasion and every day. They can be prepared in a matter of moments, with very little effort, to complement a piece of meat, poultry or game.

The basic elements

All sauces, however simple or complex, should be based on good quality ingredients. Aromatics, fresh herbs, spices, wines, alcohol, stocks – all must be chosen with the utmost care.

The barman

A sauce-maker is like a barman mixing cocktails. It is vital to get the proportions precisely right. Ingredients with a very strong flavour, like certain pungent spices, herbs and alcohol, should be used in moderation.

My sauces

From the age of fourteen, during my apprenticeship to a pâtissier, followed by many years in professional kitchens, I learnt the secret of sauces from the chefs with whom I worked. Later, I developed them to suit my own palate and created original new sauces to complement my dishes.

There are sauces to suit every season, every taste, every occasion and the time available for their preparation. My objective when making a sauce, be it savoury or sweet, is to provide the perfect accompaniment to a dish and to elevate it to gastronomic perfection – but never to dominate it.

In the course of a year at The Waterside Inn, I prepare hundreds of different sauces – modern, classic, light or unctuous, depending on the dish they are to accompany. Those in this book are among my favourites. They are creative and diverse, enormously enjoyable and perfectly accessible to the home cook.

Cooking a sauce intoxicates the senses of smell, taste and sight. The visual and odiferous pleasures it offers in its final cooking stages will tempt you to dream and discover the wonderful world of sauces.

Practical Advice

Choosing and flavouring sauces

Menu planning: Serve only one 'grand' sauce at a meal and keep the others light and simple.

• Do not serve a powerful, full-bodied sauce at the beginning of a meal.

• Try to avoid serving sauces of the same colour and texture, or with a similar base, such as wine or liqueurs.

• Do not make all the sauces at the same meal too classic or too modern. Your guests will appreciate a judicious balance.

Seasonal produce: In the same way that you would choose the finest seasonal ingredients for a finished dish, make your sauces with the best seasonal produce. The end result will be full of flavour and all the more delicious.

Seasoning: Never add too much salt to a sauce before it has reached the desired consistency and taste. Add pepper only just before serving to retain its flavour and zip.

Garlic: Always halve garlic cloves lengthways and remove the green shoot, which can be indigestible.

Mushrooms: Their wild, musky aroma of forest bark and damp earth adds a special something to many sauces. It is better to wipe fresh mushrooms clean than to wash them, as they absorb water and lose their flavour. Chop or finely slice them and add to the sauce during cooking. Some varieties, such as button or white cultivated mushrooms, tend to lack flavour, so be generous with these. Others, such as shiitake, have quite

To crush garlic, put the peeled cloves in a mortar with a good pinch of coarse salt

Crush the garlic to a paste with a pestle

an aggressive flavour and should be used sparingly. Dried mushrooms are a good substitute for fresh (soak them first), but for the ultimate pleasure, black or white truffles can be added to numerous sauces a few minutes before serving.

Shallots: Shallots become bitter after chopping, so rinse them under cold water before using in a sauce.

Vinegar and lemon: A few drops of vinegar or lemon juice added to a characterless sauce just before serving will pep up the taste.

Preparing, keeping and freezing sauces

Preparation time: The preparation times given in this book are based on ingredients which have already been weighed out and prepared as indicated in the ingredients list. They do not include the time taken to peel, chop, slice or blanch vegetables or bones, soften butter etc, or any necessary cooling time.

Cooking time: The timings given for cooking and reducing sauces are intended only as guidelines, since the degree of heat will vary depending on your hob and the type of saucepan used. The only infallible way to ensure that a sauce has reached the desired consistency is to check it on the back of a spoon.

Degreasing: The easiest way to degrease a stock is to leave it to cool completely at room temperature, then refrigerate it. The fat will solidify on the surface and can be carefully lifted off with a large spoon.

Deglazing: Liquid such as wine or stock is heated with the cooking juices and sediment left in the pan after roasting or pan-frying to make a sauce or gravy. Remove most of the fat and grease from the pan before adding the liquid.

Straining: Thin sauces can be passed straight through a conical sieve. Thicker sauces should be pushed through the sieve by pressing with the back of a ladle or twisting a small whisk.

Keeping sauces warm: A bain-marie is best for this. Use a saucepan large enough to hold the pan or bowl containing the sauce, and fill it with hot water.

Dot flakes of butter over the surface of white sauces to prevent a skin from forming. Sauces which need a liaison or 'smoothing' with butter should be kept in the bain-marie, and the liaison or butter added at the moment of serving.

Hot emulsion sauces: These sauces do not like to be kept waiting. To enjoy them at their delicate best, make them at the last possible moment and serve immediately.

Herbs and spices

In Bray, I have created a herb garden on the banks of the Thames. Every day in summer, I painstakingly and parsimoniously pick the numerous different herbs I need for my sauces and salads. Freshness is a vital factor in the success of a sauce and my herb garden is my trump card.

If you use dried herbs, keep them in airtight jars in a cool, dark place. Spices lose their colour and flavour if they are kept too long; you should throw away any open ones after 3 to 6 months because they will add nothing to your sauces and may even spoil them.

To flavour a sauce with peppercorns, crush them and place on a piece of muslin

Fold up the edges to make a purse and tie with string

The golden rules for using herbs and spices

- Use small quantities but good quality
- Do not mix contradictory and powerful flavours

If you obey these rules, you will discover a wonderful world of flavours – subtle, complex, musky, fresh, spicy and delectable.

Bouquet garni: A classic bouquet garni consists of a sprig of thyme, a bay leaf and parsley stalks wrapped and tied in a leek leaf.

Fines herbes: A mixture of fresh herbs in equal quantities: chervil, chives, parsley and tarragon. They should be snipped, not chopped, preferably just before using so that they retain all their flavour and do not become bitter.

The most popular culinary herbs are: basil, bay leaf, chervil, chives, fresh coriander, dill, fennel, garlic, horseradish, lavender, lemon grass, lemon verbena, lovage, marjoram, mint, oregano, flat or curly parsley, rosemary, sage, savory, sorrel, tarragon and thyme.

The most popular spices are: caraway, cardamom, cayenne, cinnamon, cloves, coriander seeds, cumin, curry, five-spice, ginger, juniper, mace, nutmeg, black, green, white and pink pepper, paprika, pimento, poppy seeds, saffron and star anise.

Dairy products

These play an extremely important part in sauce-making.

Crème fraîche: This can be heated to not more than 80°C, after which it will separate. To use it in a hot sauce, whisk it into the sauce off the heat, without further cooking. This slightly acidulated cream is light and refreshing and is delicious added to most cold sauces.

Double cream: This tolerates heat extremely well during cooking and can even be reduced by boiling. It is often used as a liaison, but above all it makes sauces creamy and velvety. It comes in both full and reduced-fat versions.

Hard cheeses: The most important and best are parmesan, gruyère, emmenthal and cheddar. I always buy medium-matured farmhouse cheeses, which have a full, sublime flavour. These cheeses are normally used freshly grated to finish a sauce. It takes a few minutes after they have been added for their savour to develop, so you should use them judiciously and parsimoniously at first, checking their development before adding more to the sauce. Do not use cheap, poor quality cheese, which can ruin a sauce by tasting rancid, soapy or too salty.

Roquefort: My noble Lord Roquefort will acquire star status in a salad dressing, a cold sauce for crudités and certain hot sauces. I adore roquefort. Used in moderation, it creates an explosion of different savours in a sauce. Bleu d'Auvergne and fourme d'Ambert make adequate substitutes, but cannot equal the real thing.

Unsalted butter: The finest of all dairy products, it is natural and healthy and practically indispensable in the kitchen. Its delicate taste and different complexities vary according to its provenance and origins. It adds the finishing touch to many of my sauces, but I always use it in moderation. I use only unsalted butter in my cooking. This is essential for making clarified butter (see page 21) and desirable for all sauces.

At The Waterside Inn, after many blind tastings, the butter I have chosen for the table and for my beurres blancs and sauces is the appellation contrôlée Echiré from the Deux-Sèvres. Its quality and value place it among the very best French butters.

When either unsalted or salted butter is melted, its components separate into 15 – 20% water, 4% protein, and the balance is butterfat.

Veal Stock

Veal Stock makes brown sauces delicate and well-balanced, without masking their individuality.

Makes 1 litre
Preparation time: 30 minutes
Cooking time: about 3 hours

Ingredients:

1.5 kg veal bones, chopped
¹/₂ calf's foot, split lengthways,
chopped and blanched
200 g carrots, cut into rounds
100 g onion, coarsely chopped
250 ml dry white wine
1 celery stalk, thinly sliced
6 tomatoes, peeled, deseeded
and chopped
150 g button mushrooms,
thinly sliced
2 garlic cloves
1 bouquet garni (page 11),
including a sprig of tarragon

Preheat the oven to 220°C/425°F/gas mark 7. Put the veal bones and calf's foot in a roasting pan and brown in the oven, turning them from time to time with a slotted spoon. When they have browned, add the carrots and onions, mix together and cook for another 5 minutes. Using the slotted spoon, transfer all the contents of the roasting pan to a large saucepan or casserole. Pour off the fat from the roasting pan and deglaze with the white wine, scraping up all the sediment. Set over high heat and reduce by half, then pour the wine into the saucepan. Add 3 litres cold water and bring to the boil over high heat. As soon as the liquid boils, reduce the heat so that the surface is barely trembling. Simmer for 10 minutes, then skim well and add all the other ingredients.

Simmer the stock, uncovered, for 2½ hours, skimming as necessary. Strain through a fine-mesh conical sieve into a bowl and cool over ice (see Chicken Stock, page 14).

Demi-glace or glace: Reduce the strained stock by one-third to make a demi-glace; reduce by half for a glace. These glaces enhance sauces, adding moistness and a fuller flavour. But they cannot add finesse and subtlety, since the lengthy cooking time involved destroys some of their delicate flavour and aroma.

Chicken Stock

I sometimes add half a knuckle of veal when preparing this stock, which makes it extra rich and unctuous. Like all stocks, it should be cooled as quickly as possible. The best way to do this is to plunge the saucepan into a large bowl of ice cubes until the stock is completely cold.

Ingredients:

1 boiling fowl, weighing 1.5 kg, or an equal weight of chicken carcasses or wings, blanched and refreshed

200 g carrots, cut into chunks

white part of 2 leeks, cut into chunks

1 celery stalk, coarsely chopped

1 onion, studded with 2 cloves

150 g button mushrooms, thinly sliced

1 bouquet garni (page 11)

Makes about 1.5 litres

Preparation time: **15 minutes**

Cooking time: **about 1¾ hours**

Put the chicken or carcasses in a saucepan and cover with 2.5 litres cold water. Bring to the boil over high heat, then immediately lower the heat and keep at a simmer. After 5 minutes, skim the surface and add all the other ingredients. Cook gently for 1½ hours, without boiling, skimming whenever necessary.

Strain the stock through a wire-mesh conical sieve and cool it as quickly as possible over a bowl of ice.

Chicken Velouté

This velouté can be used as a base for other sauces; just omit the sherry. Personally, I find it excellent just as it is. I serve it with poached poultry and rice or with a whole pale pan-fried veal sweetbread garnished with leaf spinach.

Ingredients:

60 g White Roux, hot (page 22)

750 ml Chicken Stock, cooled (above)

50 ml dry sherry (optional)

salt and freshly ground white pepper

Serves 6 (makes about 800 ml)

Preparation time: **5 minutes**

Cooking time: **about 30 minutes**

Put the hot white roux into a saucepan and add the cold chicken stock. Set over medium heat and bring to the boil, whisking continuously. Reduce the heat and gently simmer the velouté for 30 minutes, stirring the sauce and skimming the surface every 10 minutes. Add the sherry if you are using it, and cook for 1 more minute. Season the sauce with salt and white pepper and pass it through a wire-mesh conical sieve.

Game Stock

This stock makes the perfect sauce for pan-fried noisettes of venison. Deglaze the pan with port, add a teaspoon of redcurrant jelly, then the game stock. Whisk in a knob of butter and season to taste. Delicious!

Ingredients:

3 tbsp groundnut oil

2 kg furred or feathered game trimmings, carcasses, necks, wings etc, cut into pieces

150 g carrots, cut into rounds

150 g onions, coarsely chopped

1/2 head of garlic, halved widthways

500 ml red wine (preferably côtes du Rhône)

500 ml Veal Stock (page 12)

8 juniper berries, crushed

8 coriander seeds, crushed

1 bouquet garni (page 11), including 2 sage leaves and a celery stalk

Makes 1.5 litres

*Preparation time: **30 minutes***

Cooking time: 2¼ hours

Preheat the oven to 220°C/425°F/gas mark 7. Heat the oil in a roasting pan, then put in the game carcasses or trimmings and brown in the hot oven, turning them from time to time with a slotted spoon. When the meat has browned, add the carrots, onions and garlic, mix together and cook for another 5 minutes. With the slotted spoon, transfer all the contents of the roasting pan to a large saucepan or casserole. Pour off the fat from the roasting pan and deglaze with the red wine. Set over high heat and reduce the wine by half, then pour it into the saucepan. Add 2 litres cold water and bring to the boil over high heat. As soon as the liquid boils, reduce the heat so that the surface barely trembles. Simmer for 10 minutes, then skim well and add all the other ingredients.

Simmer the stock, uncovered, for 2 hours, skimming the surface as necessary. Strain it through a fine-mesh conical sieve into a bowl and cool as quickly as possible over a bowl of ice.

Once the stock has been strained, you can reduce it by one-third to give it more body. Like all stocks, it will keep well for several days in the fridge, or for three or four months in the freezer.

Lamb Stock

This lamb stock is light in both flavour and appearance. I use it for deglazing in many roast or pan-fried lamb recipes, such as a navarin. It can form the basis for a sauce, in which case I would flavour it with curry, star anise, mint or saffron etc to complement the dish. For a wonderful taste of spring, I sometimes use the stock to moisten a cous-cous garnished with tender young vegetables.

Ingredients:

1.5 kg scrag end, breast or lower best
end of lamb, skin and fat removed
cut into pieces
150 g carrots, cut into rounds
100 g onions, coarsely chopped
250 ml dry white wine
4 tomatoes, peeled, deseeded and
chopped
2 garlic cloves
1 bouquet garni (page 11), including
2 sprigs of tarragon and a celery stalk
6 white peppercorns, crushed

Makes 1 litre

Preparation time: **30 minutes**

Cooking time: **about 2 hours**

Preheat the oven to 220°C/425°F/gas mark 7. Put the pieces of lamb in a roasting pan and brown in the hot oven, turning them over from time to time with a slotted spoon. When the lamb has coloured, add the carrots and onions, mix together and cook for another 5 minutes. Still using the slotted spoon, transfer all the contents of the roasting pan to a large saucepan or casserole. Pour off the fat from the roasting pan, deglaze with the white wine and reduce by half. Pour the reduced wine into the saucepan, add 2.5 litres cold water and bring to the boil over high heat. As soon as the liquid boils, reduce the heat so that the surface is barely trembling. Simmer for 10 minutes, then skim the surface and add all the other ingredients.

Simmer, uncovered, for 1^{1}/$_{2}$ hours, skimming the surface as necessary. Strain the stock through a fine-mesh conical sieve into a bowl and cool it as quickly as possible over a bowl of ice.

Cooked Marinade

Large pieces of meat or game can be left in the cold marinade for one to three days; smaller pieces should be marinated for one or two hours. If you plan to serve the meat the same day, it can be placed in the marinade while this is still warm. Always use tongs or a fork to turn the meat in the marinade, never your fingers, which will spoil it.

The addition of a small amount of marinade to a game sauce will reinforce its structure and flavour.

Ingredients:

20 g butter

2 carrots, cut into rounds

2 onions, roughly chopped

1 celery stalk, thinly sliced

1 L red wine (preferably côtes du Rhône)

100 ml red wine vinegar

750 ml water

1 bouquet garni (page 11), including a sprig of rosemary

1/2 head of garlic, halved widthways

2 cloves

A pinch of crushed peppercorns

Makes 1.5 litres

(sufficient for a large piece of meat)

Preparation time: about 10 minutes

Cooking time: about 25 minutes

In a saucepan, melt the butter and sweat the vegetables for a few minutes. Add all the other ingredients and bring to the boil over high heat. Immediately lower the heat and cook gently for 20 minutes, skimming the surface whenever necessary. Unless you are going to serve the meat the same day, cool the marinade completely before using it.

Liaison techniques

Breadcrumbs

Breadcrumbs are used as a thickening agent for rustic, flavourful sauces. In country cooking, they are used to thicken the broth from a pot-au-feu or the pan juices from a roast. These are my favourite sauces when I cook at my house in Gassin in Provence.

Fresh breadcrumbs: Crumble them into the warm sauce and cook very gently for about 20 minutes, whisking occasionally. When the sauce reaches the desired consistency, serve it as it is, or pass it through a fine conical strainer.

Toasted breadcrumbs: Crumble them into a bowl, drizzle in a little olive oil and, if you like, a small quantity of ground almonds. Mix thoroughly with a fork. Add the mixture to your warm sauce and bring to the boil over low heat. Bubble gently for 5 – 10 minutes until the sauce has thickened.

Egg yolks

Sauces bound with egg yolks have a velvety texture and delicate colour. They always remind me of the creamy blanquette de veau which my mother prepared at home when I was a child.

In a bowl, break up the egg yolks with a very little barely tepid liquid: use milk, wine, chicken stock etc depending on the sauce. Off the heat, pour the yolks into the almost boiling sauce, stirring continuously with a wooden spoon. Over low heat, reheat the sauce, stirring constantly until it lightly coats the back of the spoon. It is essential not to let the sauce boil, or it will separate. As soon as it has thickened, pass it through a fine conical strainer into a clean saucepan and keep warm.

Cornflour, rice flour and arrowroot

These vegetable thickeners are quick and easy to use, need no special skill, and are ideal when you need a sauce in a hurry.

In a bowl, dissolve the thickening agent in a little cold liquid – water, milk or wine – and pour into the boiling sauce. Simmer for about 10 minutes; the sauce will thicken almost instantaneously.

Cream

Cream-thickened sauces are often used for fish, poultry, veloutés and certain soups. They add a velvet-smooth quality, which I love.

Always use double cream. You will need about 10 – 20% cream in proportion to the quantity of sauce. Boil the cream for a few minutes, then stir it into the boiling sauce.

The consistency, taste and properties of double cream vary from country to country. For example, in Britain, it is soft and delicate and can be stirred directly into the sauce and boiled without separating. In France crème fraîche is slightly acidulated and cannot easily be added uncooked to a sauce, or it will separate.

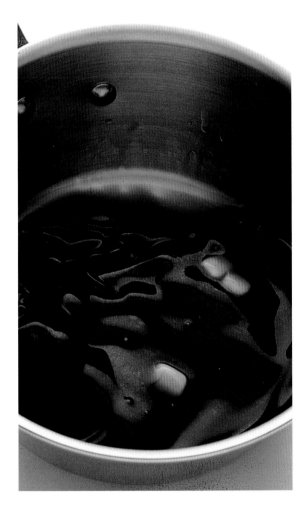

Lightening and thickening with butter

Incorporating butter into a sauce improves it in five important ways, making it lighter, smoother, glossier, thicker and mellower. Once ready, these delicate sauces must not be allowed to boil and should be served as soon as possible.

The butter should be well-chilled, almost frozen. Take the boiling sauce off the heat and incorporate small pieces of butter (5 – 10 g), one at a time. Either use a balloon whisk or hold the pan handle firmly and swirl or shake the pan from side to side, until all the butter is incorporated.

Blood

Blood is mainly used as a thickener for sauces for game, such as venison and wild boar, or in the sauce for canard au sang. I use a touch in the red wine sauce which I often serve with duck at The Waterside Inn, and also in *civet* of hare, which is a favourite dish of mine.

Blood used for cooking almost always comes from pigs, rabbit or poultry (usually chicken). It is important that it does not coagulate; a few drops of vinegar added as soon as you obtain the blood will prevent this. Allow about 150 ml blood for 1 litre of sauce, or a little more if you want a thicker sauce.

Take the almost boiling sauce off the heat and add the blood, stirring continuously with a wooden spatula. Replace the pan over medium heat and cook the sauce until it thickens, stirring all the time. As soon as the surface begins to tremble, stop the cooking and immediately pass the sauce through a fine conical strainer into another pan. Keep it warm and serve it as soon as possible.

Swirl the butter into a sauce, a small piece at a time, to lighten and thicken it

Reduction

You should be able to judge by eye when a sauce has reached the desired consistency by reduction, but it is helpful to use the back of a spoon to gauge the precise thickness. Let the sauce cool slightly before running your finger down the spoon.

Reduce the sauce over high heat to obtain the required consistency – a light juice (1), slightly syrupy (2), syrupy (3) or the very thick, rich demi-glace (5). As the sauce reduces, impurities rise to the surface (4); skim off as necessary. Never season a reduction sauce before it reaches the desired consistency.

Clarified butter

Clarified butter is used to cook meat over a high heat without blackening it. It is also used for emulsified sauces like hollandaise and its derivatives and for making brown roux. During the clarifying process, the butter loses about 20% of its original weight. To make about 100 g clarified butter, start with 120 g unsalted butter. Melt this over a very gentle heat and bring slowly to the boil. Skim off the froth from the surface. Carefully pour the liquid butter into a bowl, taking care not to include any of the milky sediment from the bottom of the pan. The clarified butter should be the colour of a light olive oil. Clarified butter will keep in the fridge for several weeks.

Beurre manié

Beurre manié is used to thicken sauces rapidly. Use only a small quantity, or the sauce will become too heavy.

It consists of two-thirds volume softened butter and one-third sifted flour, mashed together (uncooked) with a fork. Using a small whisk, incorporate small quantities of beurre manié into the sauce over high heat. The sauce will thicken immediately; let it bubble a few times, then as soon as it reaches the desired consistency, pass it through a wire-mesh conical strainer.

White Roux

This roux is classically used as a thickener in all white sauces.

Ingredients: *Makes 100 g*

50 g butter *Preparation time: 3 minutes*

50 g flour, sifted *Cooking time: 4 minutes*

Melt the butter in a heavy-based saucepan (1). Off the heat,
add the flour (2) and stir in with a small whisk or a wooden spoon
(3), then cook over medium heat for 3 minutes, stirring continuously
(4). Transfer to a bowl, cover with cling film and keep at room
temperature, or store in the fridge for several days.

Blond Roux

*This pale roux is used to thicken veloutés and sauces where
a neutral colour is required, particularly those for lamb,
veal and all poultry.*

Ingredients: *Makes 100 g*

50 g butter *Preparation time: 3 minutes*

50 g flour, sifted *Cooking time: 6 minutes*

Melt the butter in a heavy-based saucepan (1). Off the heat, add the
flour (2) and stir in with a small whisk or a wooden spoon (3), then
cook over medium heat for 5 minutes, stirring continuously. The
roux should be a rich golden colour (5). Transfer to a bowl, cover
with cling film and keep at room temperature, or store in the fridge
for several days.

Brown Roux

This roux is used to thicken many brown sauces. The clarified butter gives the sauce a deep colour without adding any of the bitterness or unpleasant flavour of burnt butter.

Makes 100 g

Preparation time: 3 minutes

Cooking time: 9 minutes

Ingredients:

50 g clarified butter (page 21)

50 g flour, sifted

Heat the clarified butter in a heavy-based saucepan. Take the pan off the heat and stir in the flour using a small whisk or a spatula. Cook the roux over medium heat for 8 minutes, stirring continuously, until it becomes chestnut-brown (left). Transfer to a bowl, cover with cling film and keep at room temperature. The roux can be stored in the fridge for several days.

Recipes

- All meats are improved and enhanced by the addition of a sauce. Some, like game, pork and rich terrines, pies and pâtés benefit from a refreshing, fruity sauce or chutney, which help to develop the flavour of the meat.
- Among my favourite sauces is that all-time great, Poivrade Sauce, whose satisfying flavour marries well with almost all red meat and game. I also adore Bigarade Sauce, which adds a new dimension to duck à l'orange.
- White sauces are the perfect complement to poached or boiled poultry, white meats and offal. Their ivory paleness, creamy whiteness or delicate blond colouring makes them appealing and easy on the eye. I particularly enjoy them in winter.
- Hot emulsion sauces are delicate and ethereal. Some, like Béarnaise Sauce are delicious enough to be eaten on their own. But remember that these sauces cannot be kept waiting, so prepare them just before serving.
- It is worth mentioning the simplest liaisons for sauces which require no recipe, such as a few caramelized onions, roasted carrots or potatoes crushed into a sauce. Garlic or shallots baked in their skins on a bed of coarse salt make a lovely thickener for lamb gravy or the sauce from a pot-roasted chicken.

Roast turkey with Buccaneer's Sauce (page 35)

Béchamel Sauce

This is the ideal sauce for any number of dishes using white meats, poultry and ham. The sauce will keep in an airtight container in the fridge for a maximum of four days.

Serves 4
*Preparation time: **5 minutes***
*Cooking time: **about 25 minutes***

Ingredients:
500 ml milk
60 g White Roux (page 22), cooled
Freshly grated nutmeg (optional)
Salt and freshly ground white pepper

Put the cold roux into a small, thick-bottomed saucepan. Bring the milk to the boil and pour it on to the roux, mixing and stirring with a whisk or wooden spatula. Set the pan over low heat and bring the mixture to the boil, still stirring continuously. As soon as it reaches boiling point, reduce the heat and cook at a very gentle simmer for about 20 minutes, stirring the sauce continuously and making sure that the whisk scrapes across all the surfaces of the pan.

Season the sauce with salt, white pepper and a very little nutmeg if you wish, then pass it through a conical strainer. You can serve it immediately or keep it warm in a bain-marie, in which case dot a few flakes of butter over the surface to prevent a skin from forming.

Classic Rich Béchamel: The old classic rich béchamel was made with the addition of veal. To make this, sweat 75 g diced veal, 30 g chopped onion, a sprig of thyme and a bay leaf in 30 g butter. In another pan make a basic béchamel and when it reaches boiling point, add the veal and onions and continue with the recipe as above.

Aurora Sauce

Hard-boiled eggs sliced into discs, coated with Aurora Sauce and browned under the grill are delicious. The sauce is also very good with poached eggs, pasta, cauliflower or grilled turkey escalopes. You can substitute a Chicken Velouté (page 14) for the Béchamel Sauce if you prefer the flavour.

Ingredients:

300 ml Béchamel Sauce (opposite)
100 ml double cream
100 ml tomato passata
20 g butter, chilled and diced
Salt and freshly ground pepper or nutmeg

Serves 6

Preparation time: **5 minutes**

Cooking time: **about 15 minutes**

Combine the béchamel and cream in a saucepan and bring to the boil over low heat, stirring continuously with a whisk. Bubble the sauce for 5 minutes, then add the tomato passata, bring the sauce back to the boil and cook for another 5 minutes, whisking continuously. Turn off the heat and whisk in the butter, a little at a time. Season the sauce with salt and pepper or nutmeg, according to taste, pass it through a wire-mesh conical sieve and serve immediately.

Bread Sauce

The perfect sauce to accompany roast chicken or turkey. It is also ideal with roast pheasant or grouse.

Ingredients:

20 g butter
60 g onion, chopped
400 ml milk
1 whole or ¹/₂ onion (weighing 60 g), studded with 2 cloves
80 g white bread, crusts removed, cubed
50 ml double cream
Salt and freshly ground white pepper

Serves 4

Preparation time: **5 minutes**

Cooking time: **about 1 hour**

Melt the butter in a small saucepan, add the chopped onion and sweat gently for 1 minute. Pour in the milk, add the clove-studded onion and simmer at about 90°C for 20 minutes. Stir in the bread and bring to the boil. Lower the heat and cook the sauce gently for 30 minutes, stirring occasionally with a wooden spoon. Remove the studded onion, add the cream and bubble the sauce gently for 5 minutes, whisking gently. Season with salt and white pepper and serve hot.

Parsley Sauce

This sauce is simplicity itself and most delicious, especially when it is prepared with the cooking liquid from a boiled ham and served with the ham. It also tastes good with plain boiled brussels sprouts, carrots or potatoes. You can enrich the sauce with cream or butter, but I prefer it without. Because it is not rich, it can be eaten with a spoon; this is why I suggest that the recipe serves four people rather than six, as you might expect.

Serves 4
Preparation time: **5 minutes**
Cooking time: **about 20 minutes**

Ingredients:

350 ml cooking liquid from a boiled ham,
*   or Chicken Stock (page 14)*
150 ml milk
40 g White Roux, cooled (page 22)
2 tbsp snipped parsley
A pinch of freshly grated nutmeg
Salt and freshly ground white pepper

Bring the cooking liquid or stock and the milk to the boil. Put the cold roux in a saucepan and pour on the hot liquid, whisking as you go. Bring to the boil over low heat, stirring continuously with the whisk as the sauce begins to bubble. Add the parsley and simmer the sauce for 15 minutes, skimming the surface with a spoon if necessary. Season with the nutmeg and salt and pepper to taste and serve piping hot.

Supreme Sauce with Sherry

A classic Supreme Sauce is made without sherry, but I think it adds a theatrical note which pleases me very much. Serve with poached poultry, sweetbreads, braised lettuce or veal escalopes. It is essential to use the best quality butter to finish this sauce.

Ingredients:

250 ml boiling Chicken Velouté (page 14)
50 g button mushrooms, thinly sliced
50 ml double cream
30 g butter, chilled and diced
4 tbsp dry sherry
Salt and freshly ground pepper

Serves 4

Preparation time: **5 minutes**

Cooking time: **about 10 minutes**

Pour the boiling chicken velouté into a saucepan and add the mushrooms and cream. Simmer over low heat for 10 minutes, stirring occasionally with a wooden spoon. Pass the sauce through a wire-mesh conical sieve into a clean saucepan, turn the heat to low and whisk in the butter, a little at a time. Turn off the heat, stir in the sherry, season the sauce with salt and pepper and serve immediately.

Soubise Sauce

Perfect for winter, this sauce goes particularly well with roast rack or loin of veal and with roast chicken or guinea fowl. It can be prepared in advance and reheated in a bain-marie.

Ingredients:

40 g butter
200 g onions, thinly sliced
1 quantity Béchamel Sauce (page 26)
150 ml double cream
Freshly grated nutmeg
Salt and freshly ground pepper

Serves 4

Preparation time: **5 minutes**

Cooking time: **25 minutes**

In a saucepan, melt the butter over low heat, add the onions and sweat for 5 minutes without colouring, stirring gently with a wooden spoon. Add the béchamel, bring to the boil over low heat and bubble gently for 10 minutes, still stirring delicately with the wooden spoon. Pass the sauce through a wire-mesh sieve into a clean saucepan, pressing the onions through with a wooden food pusher or the back of a small ladle. Add the cream and cook gently for 6 – 8 minutes, stirring continuously, until the sauce thickens to the consistency of porridge. Season to taste with nutmeg, salt and pepper and serve piping hot.

Sauce Albert

Sauce Albert, which we serve with our pot-au-feu and with cuts like silverside, veal knuckle and beef flank, is one of the legendary Roux brothers' sauces, which our faithful regulars always enjoy. It is also excellent with roast rabbit.

Ingredients:

300 ml Chicken Stock (page 14), or broth from a pot-au-feu

150 g horseradish, preferably freshly grated, or 200 g bottled horseradish, well drained

300 ml double cream

50 g fresh white bread, crusts removed, cut into small cubes

1 egg yolk

1 tsp English mustard powder, dissolved in 1 tbsp cold water

Salt and freshly ground white pepper

Serves 4

Preparation time: 15 minutes

Cooking time: about 50 minutes

Combine the chicken stock or broth and the horseradish in a small saucepan, set over medium heat and boil for 15 minutes. Add the cream and bubble gently for another 20 minutes. Transfer the sauce to a blender and whizz for 1 minute (you may have to do this in two batches), then pass the sauce through a wire-mesh conical sieve into a clean saucepan.

Add the cubes of bread and cook the sauce over low heat for 10 minutes, whisking continuously. Turn off the heat, add the egg yolk and mustard and stir for a few moments before vigorously whisking the sauce to make it very smooth; it should have the consistency of porridge. Season to taste with salt and pepper and serve at once. If you need to keep the sauce warm, do not let it boil.

Horseradish Butter

Finish a Sauce Albert with this delicious butter, or use it to pep up a Béchamel Sauce (page 26). It also goes well with any grilled white meat.

Ingredients:

50 g freshly grated horseradish

150 g butter, softened

Salt and freshly ground pepper

Makes about 200 g

Preparation time: 7 minutes

Pulverize the horseradish with a pestle in a mortar, adding the butter a little at a time. When it is all well mixed, use a plastic scraper to rub the seasoned butter through a drum sieve and season to taste with salt and pepper. Using cling film, roll it into one or two sausage shapes and refrigerate or freeze until needed.

Anchovy Butter

Use this delicious butter in Caper Sauce with Anchovies.

Ingredients:

50 g anchovy fillets in oil
150 g butter, softened
Salt and freshly ground pepper

Makes about 180 g

Preparation time: 7 minutes

Chop the anchovy fillets or pound them in a mortar. Using a wooden spoon, mix them into the butter and, using a plastic scraper, rub through a drum sieve or whizz in a food processor. Season, being circumspect with the salt, as the anchovies already contain plenty. Use cling film to roll the butter into one or two sausage shapes and refrigerate or freeze until ready to use.

Caper Sauce with Anchovies

A lively, vigorous sauce which cuts the richness of offal such as brains, sweetbreads, tripe or calf's head.

Ingredients:

500 ml Chicken Velouté (page 14)
1 bouquet garni (page 11), including
2 sprigs of savory
100 ml dry white wine
100 ml double cream
60 g Anchovy Butter (above)
30 g small capers (chop them if they are large), well drained
2 anchovy fillets, finely diced
Salt and cayenne pepper

Serves 8

Preparation time: 5 minutes

Cooking time: 15 minutes

In a saucepan, bring the velouté to the boil, add the bouquet garni and white wine and cook gently for 10 minutes. Pour in the cream and continue to cook gently for another 5 minutes. The sauce should lightly coat the back of a spoon; if it is not thick enough, increase the heat to as high as possible and reduce it for a few more minutes. Lower the heat to minimum, whisk in the anchovy butter, a little at a time, and pass the sauce through a wire-mesh conical sieve into a clean saucepan. Season with cayenne and a very little salt, stir in the capers and diced anchovies and serve at once.

Champagne Sauce with Morels

This is the Champagne Sauce which I serve with poached capon. Try this unctuous sauce for a special occasion.

Ingredients:

75 g fresh morels, or 30 g dried morels
soaked in boiling water for 1 hour
400 ml Chicken Velouté (page 14)
200 ml brut champagne
200 ml double cream
80 g Foie Gras Butter (below)
Salt and freshly ground white pepper

Serves 8

Preparation time: 10 minutes

Cooking time: 45 minutes

First clean the fresh morels. Trim the very bottom of the stalks, halve the mushrooms (or quarter them if they are very large), rinse in cold water to remove all traces of grit and delicately pat dry on a tea towel. If you are using dried morels, drain them from their soaking water and proceed as for fresh morels.

Combine the chicken velouté and three-quarters of the champagne in a saucepan and boil over medium heat for 20 minutes. Put the cream and prepared morels in another saucepan and bring to the boil over medium heat. Cook for 5 minutes, then tip the cream and morel mixture into the pan with the velouté. Cook at a bare simmer for 15 minutes, removing any skin from the surface with a spoon if necessary.

Add the remaining champagne, bubble the sauce for 2 minutes and turn off the heat. Add the foie gras butter, a little at a time, mixing it into the sauce with a wooden spoon. Season with salt and white pepper and serve immediately.

Foie Gras Butter

This creamy delicate and tasty butter gives a superb velvety finish to many sauces including Allemande, Périgueux and Port Sauces.

Ingredients:

100 g butter, softened
100 g terrine or ballotine of duck or
goose foie gras
2 tbsp armagnac or cognac
Salt and freshly ground pepper

Makes about 200 g

Preparation time: 5 minutes

Mix all the ingredients with a wooden spoon, seasoning to taste with salt and pepper. Using a plastic scraper, rub through a drum sieve or whizz in a blender. Using cling film, roll the butter into one or two sausage shapes and refrigerate or freeze until needed.

Sorrel Sauce

This sauce is one of my mother's favourites. Its hint of acidity and freshness makes it ideal for serving with pan-fried lamb chops or roast saddle of rabbit. A few shredded mint leaves added to the sauce just before serving intensify the taste of the sorrel and make the sauce more rounded.

Serves 6
Preparation time: 5 minutes
Cooking time: about 20 minutes

Ingredients:

60 g sorrel
30 g butter
40 g shallot, finely chopped
100 ml white wine
200 ml vegetable stock
200 ml double cream
Salt and freshly ground pepper

Wash the sorrel and remove the stalks. Pile up several leaves, roll them up like a cigar and shred them finely, repeating until you have shredded all the sorrel. Melt the butter in a deep frying pan, add the shallot and sweat it over low heat for 30 seconds, then put in the sorrel and sweat gently for another minute. Pour in the wine and stock and reduce the liquid by two-thirds. Add the cream and bubble for 2 minutes. The sauce should be thick enough to coat the back of a spoon lightly. Season to taste and serve immediately.

Rabbit with Sorrel Sauce

Light Chicken Gravy with Thyme

This is the best possible light gravy to accompany roast poultry. It is also good with fresh pasta and leafy vegetables.

Ingredients:

3 tbsp groundnut oil
1 kg chicken wings, coarsely chopped
100 g carrots, chopped
100 g onions, chopped
200 ml dry white wine
1 L cold water
5 juniper berries, crushed
1 garlic clove, crushed
25 g thyme, preferably fresh
Salt and freshly ground pepper

Serves 6
Preparation time: 15 minutes
Cooking time: 45–60 minutes

Heat the oil in a deep frying pan, put in the chicken wings and fry over high heat until golden brown, stirring occasionally with a wooden spoon. Pour off the oil and the fat released by the chicken, then add the carrots and onions. Stir with a wooden spoon and sweat gently for 3 minutes. Pour in the white wine and reduce the liquid by half. Add all the other ingredients, being sparing with the salt and pepper, and bubble the sauce gently for 45 minutes, skimming as often as necessary. Pass it through a conical sieve; it is now ready to serve. For a more concentrated flavour, reduce the sauce over medium heat.

Zingara Sauce

Serve this fine, delicate sauce with pan-fried or grilled poultry or with veal escalopes, chops or scallopine.

Ingredients:

400 ml Veal Stock (page 12)
1 tbsp tomato passata
30 g butter
60 g button mushrooms, cut into batons
50 ml dry white wine
30 g lean ham, cut into batons
30 g cooked ox tongue, cut into batons
40 g fresh or preserved truffle, cut into batons
30 ml best quality madeira
Salt and cayenne pepper

Serves 6
Preparation time: 10 minutes
Cooking time: about 35 minutes

Put the stock and tomato passata in a saucepan, reduce by two-thirds over medium heat, then pass through a wire-mesh conical sieve into a bowl. In another saucepan, melt the butter, add the mushrooms and sweat them gently for 30 seconds. Pour in the white wine and reduce it almost completely. Add the ham, tongue and truffle, mix delicately with a wooden spoon, then pour in the madeira and cook at a bare simmer for 2 minutes. Add the reduced veal stock and simmer for another 5 minutes. Season the sauce to taste with salt and cayenne and serve at once.

Buccaneer's Sauce

Serve this sauce with veal chops, or roast veal, chicken or turkey (picture page 24). If you like, garnish with slices of banana pan-fried in butter.

Ingredients:

40 g fresh ginger, peeled and grated
60 g shallots or small onions, thinly sliced
100 g banana, peeled and cut into rounds
100 g butter
6 tbsp raspberry vinegar
400 ml Veal Stock (page 12)
Salt and freshly ground black pepper

Serves 8

Preparation time: **10 minutes**
Cooking time: **about 25 minutes**

Melt half the butter in a saucepan, add the shallots or onions and sweat for 1 minute over medium heat. Add the ginger and cook until very lightly coloured, stirring continuously. Still stirring, add the banana rounds and cook over low heat for 2 minutes, until the banana softens and begins to disintegrate. Immediately, add the raspberry vinegar and cook very gently for another 2 minutes, still stirring.

Peach Sauce

I serve this delicate, fruity sauce with roast pigeon or with a young duckling. For preference, make the sauce with white peaches.

Ingredients:

30 g butter
30 g caster sugar
2 very ripe medium peaches, peeled and cut into cubes
20 ml cognac
3 tbsp red wine vinegar
100 ml red wine, preferably Burgundy
1 clove
1 1/2 tsp fennel seeds
300 ml Veal Stock (page 12)
40 g butter, chilled and diced
Salt and freshly ground pepper

Serves 4

Preparation time: **10 minutes**
Cooking time: **about 1 hour**

Melt the butter in a deep frying pan, add the sugar and stir with a wooden spoon. As soon as the sugar has caramelized and begun to colour lightly, put in the peach cubes and increase the heat. Cook, stirring continuously, until the peaches have almost collapsed into a purée. Add the cognac, then, after 30 seconds, the vinegar. After 1 more minute, pour in the wine and add the clove and fennel seeds.

Bring to the boil and cook gently for 10 minutes, skimming the surface with a slotted spoon as necessary. Pour in the veal stock and cook the sauce for about 30 minutes, until it coats the back of a spoon. Pass it through a conical sieve, whisk in the butter, a little at a time, season to taste and serve immediately.

Périgueux Sauce

This sauce is excellent served with little hot pies or pâtés en croûte, with beef tournedos or pan-fried saddle of lamb, and of course on pasta. For a richer sauce, substitute 50 g Foie Gras Butter (page 32) for the 40 g chilled butter.

Serves 6
Preparation time: 5 minutes
Cooking time: about 30 minutes

Ingredients:

400 ml Veal Stock (page 12)
50 ml bottled truffle juice, or (preferably)
the cooking juice from fresh truffles
20 g truffles, finely chopped
40 g butter, well chilled and diced
Salt and freshly ground pepper

Use the juice from freshly cooked or preserved truffles

Finely chop the truffles

In a small saucepan, reduce the veal stock over medium heat (1) until it forms a veil and lightly coats the bowl of a spoon (2). Add the truffle juice and cook for another 5 minutes. Add the chopped truffles and give the sauce a bubble. Take the pan off the heat and add the butter, one piece at a time, swirling and rotating the pan to incorporate it (3). Season the sauce with salt and pepper to taste and serve immediately (4).

Périgourdine Sauce: You can replace the chopped truffles with truffles sliced into discs or 'turned' into olive shapes. The sauce is then known as Périgourdine.

Light Lamb Gravy Scented with Lavender Honey

This is a lovely sauce to serve with grilled lamb chops or a roast leg of lamb. Or do as we did as children – make a well in the middle of a pile of mashed potatoes and pour in a few spoonfuls of gravy.

Ingredients:

4 tbsp groundnut oil

1 kg neck or scrag end of lamb on the bone, coarsely chopped

50 g honey, preferably lavender

100 g carrots, coarsely chopped

100 g onions, coarsely chopped

200 ml red wine

1.25 L water

1 bouquet garni (page 11)

6 peppercorns, crushed

1 marmande tomato, peeled, deseeded and chopped

1 garlic clove, crushed

Salt and freshly ground pepper

Serves 8

Preparation time: **15 minutes**

Cooking time: **1¼ hours**

Heat the oil in a deep frying pan, put in the lamb and fry briskly until browned all over. Pour off the oil and the fat released by the lamb. Using a palette knife, spread the honey over the pieces of lamb, then add the carrots and onions to the pan. Stir with a wooden spoon and sweat gently for 3 minutes. Deglaze with the red wine and cook over medium heat for 5 minutes. Add the rest of the ingredients, being sparing with the salt and pepper, and bubble the sauce gently for 1 hour, skimming the surface whenever necessary. Pass it through a conical sieve; it is now ready to serve as it is, but for a more concentrated aroma, reduce the sauce for a little longer.

The sauce will keep in an airtight container in the fridge for a few days, or for several weeks in the freezer.

Bigarade Sauce

I love this sauce served with slices of pan-fried calf's liver or sliced grilled kidneys. For a classic sauce for duck à l'orange, I add some duck wings (when I can get them), which I brown quickly before adding them to the sauce along with the veal stock at the beginning of cooking.

Ingredients:

45 g caster sugar

3 tbsp red wine vinegar

700 ml Veal Stock (page 12)

300 g duck wings (optional)

Juice of 3 oranges

Juice of 1 lemon

Zest of 2 oranges, cut into fine julienne and blanched

Zest of the lemon, cut into fine julienne and blanched

Salt and freshly ground pepper

Serves 6

*Preparation time: **10 minutes***

*Cooking time: **about 50 minutes***

Put the sugar and vinegar in a deep frying pan and cook over a very low heat to make a deep golden caramel. Immediately pour in the veal stock and orange and lemon juice and bring to the boil. Lower the heat and cook gently for 45 minutes, skimming the surface whenever necessary. The sauce should now be thick enough to coat the back of a spoon lightly. If it is not, cook for a little longer. Pass the sauce through a conical sieve, season to taste with salt and pepper, then add the orange and lemon zests and serve. If you are not serving the sauce immediately, keep it warm in a bain-marie without adding the zests and add them only at the last moment.

Five-spice Sauce

This sauce is excellent with a chicken baked in a salt crust, or with pan-fried veal tournedos served with pilaff rice.

Ingredients:

250 g chicken wings, blanched, refreshed and drained
2 tbsp groundnut oil
60 g carrots, chopped
60 g onions, chopped
50 ml white wine vinegar
400 ml Chicken Stock (page 14)
80 g tomatoes, peeled, deseeded and chopped
1 small bouquet garni (page 11), including a sprig of tarragon
100 ml double cream
1 tsp five-spice powder
Salt and freshly ground pepper

Serves 4
Preparation time: 20 minutes
Cooking time: about 30 minutes

Put the chicken wings and oil in a shallow pan and brown over high heat. Pour off the oil and fat from the chicken, then add the carrots and onions to the pan (1) and sweat them for 2 minutes. Off the heat, sprinkle on the vinegar (2) and leave for 1 minute. Add the chicken stock, tomatoes and bouquet garni, bring to the boil, then cook over low heat, skimming the surface whenever necessary, until the sauce lightly coats the bowl of a spoon (3). Add the cream and five-spice powder (left) and bubble gently for 2 minutes. Pass the sauce through a wire-mesh conical sieve and season to taste. Keep it warm in a bain-marie or serve immediately.

Curry Sauce

Serve this creamy, slightly fruity sauce with simply grilled veal escalopes or chicken, garnished with curried or pilaff rice.

Ingredients:

40 g butter

60 g onion, chopped

300 g pineapple, cut into small pieces

1 medium banana, cut into rounds

1 dessert apple (preferably a Cox),
washed and cut into small pieces

40 g curry powder

2 tbsp grated fresh or desiccated coconut

300 ml Veal Stock (page 12)

200 ml coconut milk

Salt

Serves 8

Preparation time: **10 minutes**

Cooking time: **about 30 minutes**

Melt the butter in a saucepan, add the onion and sweat over low heat for 1 minute. Add the pineapple, banana and apple and cook gently for 5 minutes, stirring with a wooden spoon. Add the curry and grated coconut, then pour in the veal stock and coconut milk. Bring to the boil and bubble the sauce gently for 20 minutes. Pass it through a wire-mesh conical sieve, season with salt to taste and serve immediately. If you wish, you can keep the sauce warm in a bain-marie; dot the surface with a few flakes of butter to prevent a skin from forming.

Bordelaise Sauce

This wonderful sauce looks as good as it tastes. It is delectable with any cut of beef, such as entrecôte, ribs or sirloin.

Ingredients:

40 g shallots, finely chopped

8 white peppercorns, crushed

200 ml claret

300 ml Veal Stock (page 12)

1 small bouquet garni (page 11)

200 – 400 g beef marrow (according to
taste), soaked in iced water

30 g butter, chilled and diced

Salt and freshly ground pepper

Serves 4

Preparation time: **10 minutes**

Cooking time: **about 30 minutes**

Put the shallots, peppercorns and claret in a saucepan and reduce over high heat by one-third. Add the stock and bouquet garni and bubble gently for 20 minutes, or until the sauce coats the back of a spoon. Pass it through a fine conical sieve into another saucepan. Drain the beef marrow and cut it into small pieces or rounds. Place in a small saucepan, cover with a little cold water and salt lightly. Set over medium heat and bring to the boil. Immediately turn off the heat, leave the marrow for 30 seconds, then drain it well. Season the sauce to taste, whisk in the butter, add the beef marrow and serve.

Aubergine Sauce with Tarragon

Serve this creamy, refreshing sauce with roast rabbit, veal or pork chops, or a dish of wide noodles.

Ingredients:

2 tbsp olive oil
60 g shallots, finely chopped
150 g aubergine
50 ml red wine
300 ml Veal Stock (page 12)
2 tbsp double cream
A large pinch of paprika
1 tbsp wholegrain mustard
1 tbsp snipped tarragon
Salt

Serves 4

*Preparation time: **10 minutes***
*Cooking time: **about 25 minutes***

Cut the aubergine into cubes (do not peel it). Salt lightly, leave for 5 minutes to draw out any bitterness, then pat dry. Heat the oil in a saucepan, then put in the shallots and aubergine. Cook over medium heat, stirring with a wooden spoon, until the aubergine begins to soften. Add the wine and cook for 3 minutes. Pour in the veal stock and bubble gently for 15 minutes. Add the cream and a generous pinch of paprika, then transfer the sauce to a blender and whizz for 30 seconds. Pass the sauce through a wire-mesh conical sieve into another saucepan, add the mustard and tarragon and bring back to the boil. Season to taste with salt and serve at once.

Venison Sauce with Blackberries

This fragrant, satisfying but not overly rich sauce is ideal with a roast saddle or gigot of venison.

Ingredients:

150 g blackberries
30 g caster sugar
2 tbsp red wine vinegar
600 ml Game Stock (page 15)
Dried zest of 1/2 orange
1/2 cinnamon stick
50 ml Banyuls wine
60 g butter, well chilled and diced
Salt and freshly ground pepper

Serves 6

*Preparation time: **10 minutes***
*Cooking time: **about 40 minutes***

Put the blackberries and sugar in a saucepan and cook over low heat, stirring with a wooden spoon until the blackberries have collapsed into a purée. Turn off the heat, add the vinegar, give a stir, then pour in the game stock. Add the dried orange zest and cinnamon, bring to the boil, then simmer gently for 25 minutes, skimming the surface whenever necessary. Add the wine and cook for a further 5 minutes, then pass the sauce through a wire-mesh conical sieve into another saucepan. Whisk in the butter, a little at a time, season the sauce with salt and pepper and serve at once.

Charcutière Sauce

A childhood memory...This homely sauce accompanied the pork chops and mashed potatoes which our grandfather and father served at their charcuterie in Charolles. If there was any left over, they would serve it to us the next day with a dish of wide noodles. I prefer this rather piquant sauce to have a slightly thick consistency, which I think complements the texture of pork.

Serves 4

Preparation time: *5 minutes*

Cooking time: *about 20 minutes*

Ingredients:

30 g butter

60 g onion, finely chopped

100 ml dry white wine

300 ml Veal Stock (page 12)

1 tbsp strong Dijon mustard

40 g beurre manié (page 21)

30 g cornichons, cut into long, thin strips

Salt and freshly ground pepper

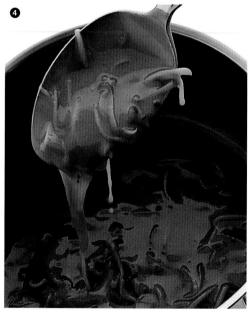

In a small saucepan, melt 30 g butter, add the onions and sweat gently without colouring for 1 minute. Pour in the wine (1) and reduce by half over medium heat. Add the veal stock (2) and bubble the sauce gently until it is thick enough to coat the bowl of a spoon. Whisk in the mustard and the beurre manié, a little at a time (3), and cook for another 2 minutes. Season to taste with salt and pepper. Pass the sauce through a conical sieve into a small saucepan containing the strips of cornichon (4) and serve it immediately, or keep it warm for a few minutes in a bain-marie set over low heat.

Juniper Sauce

This sauce is simple but highly scented, with a hint of muskiness. It is perfect with grilled or pan-fried steaks or lightly cooked game, such as pan-fried fillets of hare or medallions of venison.

Ingredients:

40 g shallots, chopped

200 ml red wine, preferably côtes du Rhône

300 ml Veal Stock (page 12)

14 juniper berries, crushed

2 tbsp redcurrant jelly

40 g butter, chilled and diced

Salt and freshly ground pepper

Serves 6

*Preparation time: **5 minutes***

*Cooking time: **about 25 minutes***

Put the shallot and wine in a saucepan, set over medium heat and reduce the wine by one-third. Add the veal stock, then the juniper berries and bubble gently for 15 minutes. Stir in the redcurrant jelly and, as soon as it has dissolved, pass the sauce through a wire-mesh conical sieve into a clean pan. Whisk in the butter, a little at a time, season to taste with salt and pepper and serve immediately.

Morel Sauce

Truly one for mushroom lovers, this sauce is excellent served with pan-fried medallions of veal or fresh pasta. You can substitute button mushrooms for the morels, but of course the flavour will not be as fine.

Ingredients:

40 g butter

40 g shallot, chopped

250 g fresh morels, finely sliced, or 75 g dried morels, infused in boiling water for 10 minutes, then finely sliced

300 ml Chicken Stock (page 14)

350 ml double cream

60 g cooked or tinned duck or goose foie gras

Salt and freshly ground pepper

Serves 8

*Preparation time: **10 minutes***

*Cooking time: **about 25 minutes***

Melt the butter in a thick-bottomed saucepan. Add the shallot, then the morels and sweat gently for 5 minutes. Add the chicken stock and cook over medium heat for 5 minutes. Next add the cream and, still over medium heat, reduce the sauce by one-third, stirring occasionally with a wooden spoon. Transfer to a blender and process for 5 minutes. Pass the sauce through a conical sieve back into the saucepan, set over low heat and whisk in the foie gras, a small piece at a time. Season with salt and pepper and serve immediately or, if necessary, keep it warm on a very low heat for a few minutes.

Chasseur Sauce

This light savoury sauce is quick to make. It goes very well with poultry and veal.

Ingredients:

200 g button mushrooms
100 g butter
40 g shallots, finely chopped
400 ml dry white wine
400 ml Veal Stock (page 12)
1 tbsp snipped flat-leaf parsley
1 tsp snipped tarragon
Salt and freshly ground black pepper

Serves 8

Preparation time: **10 minutes**
Cooking time: **about 20 minutes**

Wipe the mushrooms clean and slice them finely and evenly. Heat half the butter in a shallow pan, add the mushrooms and cook over medium heat for 1 minute. Add the shallots and cook for 1 more minute, taking care not to let it colour.

Tip the mixture into a fine-mesh conical sieve to drain off the cooking butter. Put it back into the shallow pan, add the wine and reduce it by half over medium heat. Pour in the veal stock and cook gently for 10 – 15 minutes, until the sauce is thick enough to coat the back of a spoon. Take the pan off the heat and whisk in the remaining butter and the snipped herbs. Season to taste with salt and pepper.

Savory and Tapenade Sauce

This sauce is very fluid, almost like a jus, and bursting with the Provençal flavours of savory and olives. I often serve it with pan-fried or roast saddle, shoulder or leg of lamb. If you happen to have some lamb stock, substitute it for the veal stock.

Ingredients:

100 ml dry white wine
40 g shallots, chopped
15 g savory
6 white peppercorns, crushed
200 ml Veal Stock (page 12)
60 g black or green tapenade (olive paste)
30 g butter, chilled and diced
Salt and freshly ground pepper

Serves 4

Preparation time: **5 minutes**
Cooking time: **about 25 minutes**

Combine the wine, shallots, savory and crushed peppercorns in a small saucepan, set over medium heat and reduce the wine by half. Pour in the veal stock, reduce the heat to very low and simmer gently for 20 minutes. Whisk in the tapenade, then, still over the lowest possible heat, whisk in the butter, a little at a time. Season the sauce with salt and pepper, pass it through a wire-mesh conical sieve and serve at once.

Exotic Sauce

This fruity, refreshing sauce has a light spiciness. It is particularly good with sautéed chicken or rabbit.

Ingredients:

1 very ripe mango
2 passion fruit
2 tbsp cognac or armagnac
200 ml Veal Stock (page 12)
100 ml double cream
4 drops of tabasco
Salt and freshly ground pepper

Serves 4

Preparation time: 5 minutes

Cooking time: about 15 minutes

Using a small knife with a flexible blade, peel the mango and cut off the flesh around the stone. Finely dice the flesh and place in a small saucepan. Halve the passion fruit, scoop the seeds into the saucepan (1) and add the alcohol. Cook over low heat for 5 minutes, then add the veal stock (2) and cook for another 5 minutes. Pour in the cream, add the tabasco (3) and bubble the sauce for 5 minutes, then transfer to a blender and whizz for 1 minute. Pass the sauce through a wire-mesh conical sieve into a small saucepan (4), season to taste with salt and pepper and serve immediately, or keep it warm for a few minutes in a bain-marie.

Vineyard Sauce with Spices

Serve this sauce with roast pheasant or partridge garnished with grapes. If you prefer, substitute veal stock for game stock.

Ingredients:

24 grapes, peeled and deseeded
50 g caster sugar
50 ml armagnac or cognac
300 ml red wine, preferably côtes du Rhône
500 ml Game Stock (page 15)
1 tsp five-spice powder
1 small bouquet garni (page 11),
including 2 sage leaves
50 g butter, well chilled and diced
Salt and freshly ground pepper

Serves 6

Preparation time: 15 minutes

Cooking time: about 45 minutes

Put the grapes and sugar in a saucepan, set over medium heat and cook, stirring every minute with a wooden spoon, until the grapes have disintegrated into a lightly caramelized compote. Add the alcohol and ignite it, then pour in the wine and reduce by one-third. Add all the other ingredients and simmer for 30 minutes, or until the sauce coats the back of a spoon, skimming the surface whenever necessary. Pass the sauce through a wire-mesh conical sieve, season with salt and pepper, then whisk in the chilled butter, a little at a time. Serve immediately.

Light Chicken Sauce with Curaçao

This sauce has a very light consistency, almost like a thin gravy. I like to serve it with roast or pan-fried poussin or pigeon.

Ingredients:

2 tbsp groundnut oil

250 g chicken wings and necks, blanched, refreshed and drained

60 g shallots, diced

80 g carrots, diced

60 g celery, diced

4 star anise, coarsely chopped

30 ml curaçao

200 ml Chicken Stock (page 14)

200 ml Veal Stock (page 12)

30 g butter, chilled and diced

Salt and freshly ground pepper

Serves 4

Preparation time: **5 minutes**

Cooking time: **about 30 minutes**

Heat the oil in a deep frying pan, put in the chicken wings and necks and quickly brown them all over. Pour off the oil and fat rendered by the chicken, then add the diced vegetables to the chicken in the pan, together with the star anise and sweat everything gently for 2 minutes.

Add the curaçao, cook for 1 minute, then pour in the chicken stock, increase the heat to high and reduce the stock by half. Add the veal stock and simmer the sauce gently for another 20 minutes. Pass it through a wire-mesh conical sieve into a clean pan, whisk in the butter a little at a time, season to taste with salt and pepper and serve immediately.

Devil Sauce

This robust, highly scented sauce goes very well with all grilled poultry, particularly spatchcocked poussin or chicken.

Ingredients:

30 ml best quality red wine vinegar

100 ml dry white wine

20 white peppercorns, crushed

50 g shallots, chopped

1 bouquet garni (page 11), including 2 sprigs of tarragon

400 ml Veal Stock (page 12)

40 g butter, chilled and diced

1 tbsp snipped chervil or flat-leaf parsley

Serves 4

Preparation time: **5 minutes**

Cooking time: **about 45 minutes**

Combine the vinegar, white wine, crushed white peppercorns, shallots and bouquet garni in a saucepan. Set over medium heat and reduce the liquid by four-fifths. Pour in the veal stock and bubble gently for about 20 minutes, or until the sauce is thick enough to coat the back of a spoon. Pass it through a wire-mesh sieve into a clean saucepan and whisk in the butter, a little at a time. Season to taste with salt and pepper and add the chervil or parsley just before serving.

Cherry Tomato Sauce

This sauce is delicious served not only with pasta, but also with many grilled white meats. I greedily sup it with a spoon. It can be reheated very successfully and will keep in an airtight container in the fridge for several days.

Ingredients:

1 kg very ripe cherry tomatoes,
stalks removed

1 tsp caster sugar

1 tbsp snipped basil leaves

30 ml ruby port

3 tbsp olive oil

60 g onion, chopped

80 g celery, chopped

6 thick slices of bacon (about 120 g),
de-rinded and diced

6 drops of tabasco

1 tsp worcestershire sauce

Juice of $1/2$ lemon

Salt and freshly ground pepper

Serves 8

Preparation time: **15 minutes**

Cooking time: **about 1 hour**

Preheat the oven to 160°C/320°F/gas mark 3.

Put the tomatoes into an ovenproof earthenware or enamel casserole with a lid and add the sugar, basil, port and a little salt. Cover and cook in the oven for about 45 minutes, until the tomatoes have collapsed into a purée.

Meanwhile, combine the olive oil, onion, celery and bacon in a saucepan and set over medium heat. Cook for about 20 minutes, stirring frequently with a wooden spoon, until everything is pale golden and well softened. Spoon off the excess oil, then mix the contents of the saucepan with the tomatoes. Transfer to a blender and whizz for 1 minute. Pass the sauce through a wire-mesh conical sieve into another saucepan and add the tabasco, worcestershire sauce, lemon juice and salt and pepper to taste. Simmer the sauce for another 5 minutes, then serve immediately.

Béarnaise Sauce

This sauce is wonderful with grilled steak and beef fondue. I often eat it just on its own, spread on a piece of bread.

Ingredients:

2 tbsp white wine vinegar

3 tbsp snipped tarragon

30 g shallot, finely chopped

10 peppercorns, crushed

4 egg yolks

3 tbsp cold water

250 g freshly clarified butter (page 21), cooled to tepid

2 tbsp snipped chervil

Juice of $1/2$ lemon

Salt and freshly ground pepper

Serves 6

*Preparation time: **20 minutes***

*Cooking time: **12 – 15 minutes***

Combine the vinegar, 2 tbsp tarragon, the shallot and peppercorns in a small, thick-bottomed saucepan, and reduce by half over low heat. Set aside in a cool place. When the vinegar reduction is cold, add the egg yolks and cold water. Set the pan over low heat and whisk continuously, making sure that the whisk reaches right down into the bottom of the pan. As you whisk, gently increase the heat; the sauce should emulsify slowly and gradually, becoming unctuous after 8 – 10 minutes. Do not let it become hotter than 65°C.

Turn off the heat and whisk the clarified butter into the sauce, a little at a time. Season with salt and pepper and pass the sauce through a wire-mesh conical sieve into another pan. Stir in the rest of the tarragon, the chervil and lemon juice and serve at once.

Paloise Sauce

This is basically a Béarnaise Sauce flavoured with mint instead of tarragon. It is excellent with roast or grilled lamb, and often appears on the menu at The Waterside Inn.

Ingredients:

1 quantity Béarnaise Sauce (above), made without tarragon

1 tbsp snipped mint leaves

Grilled lamb cutlets with Paloise Sauce

Serves 6

*Preparation time: **20 minutes***

*Cooking time: **12 – 15 minutes***

Follow the recipe for Béarnaise Sauce, substituting two-thirds of the mint for the tarragon. Pass the sauce through a wire-mesh conical sieve, then add the lemon juice, chervil and the remaining mint. Serve immediately.

Parsley Coulis

*This coulis is delicious served with a grilled veal escalope or chicken breast.
I sometimes substitute a pinch of curry powder for the pepper.*

Serves 8

Preparation time: 10 minutes

Cooking time: 8 – 10 minutes

Ingredients:

*400 g curly or flat-leaf parsley,
stalks removed*

300 ml double cream

50 g shallots, thinly sliced

100 ml milk, at boiling point

Salt and freshly ground pepper

Wash the parsley in plenty of cold water. Bring a pan of lightly salted water to the boil and plunge in the parsley (1). Boil for 2 minutes, then refresh in iced water (2), drain, put the parsley in a cloth (3) and squeeze the parsley to eliminate all the water (4).

In a saucepan, boil the cream with the shallots and reduce by one-third. Add the parsley (5) and bubble for 2 minutes, stirring continuously with a wooden spoon. Take the pan off the heat, add the boiling milk and stir. Purée in a blender for 2 – 3 minutes, until very smooth, then rub through a drum sieve (6), using a plastic scraper. Season with salt and pepper and serve hot, but do not boil the coulis once it has been sieved.

Port Sauce

One of my favourite simple game dishes is pan-fried pheasant breasts served with this light sauce. It is also excellent with pan-fried venison cutlets and roast partridge. For preference, I would use blackcurrants, but since their season is short, I also use cranberries. These give the sauce a very slightly bitter tinge which is refreshing and very digestible.

Ingredients:

60 g butter

60 g shallots, very finely sliced

100 g button mushrooms, finely sliced

50 g blackcurrants or cranberries

250 ml red port, at least 10 years old

Dried zest of 1/4 orange

300 ml Veal Stock (page 12)
or Game Stock (page 15)

Salt and freshly ground pepper

Serves 4

Preparation time: **10 minutes**

Cooking time: **30 minutes**

Melt half the butter in a small saucepan. Add the shallots and sweat until soft, then add the mushrooms and cranberries or blackcurrants and cook gently for 3 – 4 minutes. Pour in the port, add the orange zest and reduce by one-third. Add the stock and simmer for 25 minutes, skimming the surface whenever necessary. Pass the sauce through a conical sieve, swirl in the rest of the butter, shaking and rotating the pan, then season to taste with salt and pepper.

Apple Sauce

Apple sauce is delicious served with young wild boar, wild duck, roast partridge and pheasant or roast pork.

Ingredients:

500 g dessert apples, preferably Cox

150 ml water

20 g caster sugar

Juice of 1/2 lemon

1/2 cinnamon stick, or a pinch of ground cinnamon

30 g butter

A pinch of salt

Serves 6

Preparation time: **5 minutes**

Cooking time: **about 15 minutes**

Peel and core the apples and dice them finely. Place in a thick-bottomed saucepan together with all the other ingredients except the butter and salt. Set over medium heat, cover and cook for about 15 minutes, until the apples are tender but not dried out. Take the pan off the heat and, with a small whisk, whisk in the butter and a pinch of salt to make a very smooth compote. The consistency of the sauce will vary according to how ripe or green the apples are. If it seems too thick, add a tablespoon of water. Remove the cinnamon stick before serving.

Rich Pomerol Sauce

This rich, profound and complex sauce is perfect with roast saddle of hare or a well-marinated roast gigot of young wild boar. The perfect accompaniments to these regal game dishes are späetzle noodles, chestnuts and braised celeriac.

Ingredients:

300 ml top quality pomerol wine

1 quantity Poivrade Sauce (page 60), without the added butter

20 g bitter chocolate (at least 70% cocoa solids), melted

75 g Foie Gras Butter (page 32)

Salt and freshly ground pepper

Serves 6

Preparation time: **10 minutes**

Cooking time: **about 25 minutes**

Pour the wine into a saucepan and reduce it by one-third. Add the poivrade sauce and simmer gently for 15 minutes, then whisk in the melted chocolate. Bubble the sauce for 30 seconds, then turn off the heat and whisk in the foie gras butter, a little at a time. Pass the sauce through a wire-mesh conical sieve, season with salt and pepper and serve at once.

Arabica Fig Sauce

This sauce is excellent with roast wild duck or wood pigeon. Fresh figs poached in red wine make a wonderful garnish. Be careful not to boil the sauce after adding the coffee, or it will become slightly bitter.

Ingredients:

6 very ripe fresh figs, each cut into 6 pieces

100 ml ruby port

400 ml Game Stock (page 15)

6 black peppercorns, crushed

1 tbsp instant coffee powder, dissolved in 1 tbsp water

40 g butter, chilled and diced

Salt and freshly ground pepper

Serves 8

Preparation time: **10 minutes**

Cooking time: **about 40 minutes**

Put the figs and port in a saucepan and simmer gently for 5 minutes. Pour in the game stock, add the crushed peppercorns and bubble gently for 25 minutes, skimming the surface from time to time. Add the coffee, then immediately turn off the heat. Pour the sauce into a blender, whizz for 30 seconds, then pass it through a wire-mesh conical sieve and whisk in the butter, one piece at a time. Season to taste with salt and pepper and serve immediately.

Pumpkin Sauce with Sweet Spices

This fruity sauce with its delicate flavour of spices is perfect with fillets of wild rabbit, noisettes of young wild boar or pan-fried breast of wild duck served with a light garlic-flavoured potato purée and crisply cooked mange-tout.

Ingredients:

500 g game trimmings or chopped game carcasses
3 tbsp oil
60 g shallots, finely chopped
300 g pumpkin flesh, cut into small cubes
50 ml raspberry vinegar
200 ml sweet white wine (sauternes or barsac)
500 ml vegetable stock
1 bouquet garni (page 11)
1 vanilla pod, split lengthways
3 star anise
40 g butter, well chilled and diced
Salt and freshly ground pepper

Serves 4

*Preparation time: **20 minutes***
*Cooking time: **about 1½ hours***

Heat the oil in a deep frying pan, add the game trimmings or carcasses and briskly brown them all over. Pour off the oil and fat released by the game, then put in the shallots and pumpkin and sweat them gently over low heat for 3 minutes. Turn off the heat and add the raspberry vinegar. After 1 minute, deglaze with the white wine and simmer for 5 minutes, then add the vegetable stock, bouquet garni and spices and cook very gently for 45 minutes, skimming the surface whenever necessary.

Pass the sauce through a wire-mesh conical sieve into a clean pan and reduce until it coats the back of a spoon. Off the heat, whisk in the butter, a little at a time. Season to taste with salt and pepper and serve the sauce at once.

Poivrade Sauce

This sauce should be made with the marinade you have used for the game the sauce is to accompany. Poivrade Sauce is rich and powerful and perfect for a large piece of game, such as a haunch of venison, saddle of young wild boar or roast chump of hare. It can also be served with pan-fried noisettes of venison. As these are delicate, you should not swamp the flavour with a very full-bodied sauce, so use only half the given quantity of marinade and do not reduce the sauce too much.

Serves 6

Preparation time: *20 minutes*

Cooking time: *about 1¼ hours*

Ingredients:

3 tbsp oil

500 g trimmings of furred game
(eg venison, hare, wild boar),
cut into pieces

100 g carrots, chopped

80 g onions, chopped

30 ml red wine vinegar

200 ml Cooked Marinade (page 17)

500 ml Veal Stock (page 12)
or Game Stock (page 15)

1 bouquet garni (page 11)

6 peppercorns, crushed

40 g butter, chilled and diced

Salt and freshly ground pepper

Heat the oil in a deep frying pan, put in the game trimmings (1) and brown them over high heat (2). Strain off the oil and fat released by the cooking, add the chopped carrot and onion to the pan and sweat over low heat for 3 minutes (3). Pour in the vinegar and marinade and cook over medium heat for 5 minutes. Add the stock and bouquet garni (4) and cook at a bare simmer for 45 minutes, then add the crushed peppercorns and cook for a further 10 minutes.

Strain the sauce through a conical sieve into a small saucepan. Off the heat, swirl in the butter, a little at a time, until the sauce is smooth and glossy. Season to taste and serve at once, or keep the sauce warm, taking care not to let it boil. If you are going to do this, add the butter only at the last moment.

Grand Veneur Sauce: Add 2 teaspoons redcurrant jelly and 2 tablespoons double cream to the Poivrade Sauce to make a Grand Veneur Sauce (this means 'Master of the King's Hunt').

Quick Sauce for Game Birds

This quickly prepared but serious sauce is not too robust, but since it absorbs the savour of the carcasses during its brief cooking, it retains the full flavour of the game birds.

Ingredients:

2 wild duck, or 2 snipe,
or 4 wood pigeons
50 ml cognac or armagnac
150 ml red wine
450 ml vegetable stock
5 juniper berries, crushed
1 sprig of thyme
1/2 bay leaf
4 tbsp double cream
Salt and freshly ground pepper

Serves 4

Preparation time: **5 minutes**

Cooking time: **about 30 minutes**

Roast the game birds until they are cooked to your liking, then remove the thighs and breasts, wrap them in foil and keep them warm until ready to eat.

Chop the carcasses, place in a saucepan and heat them through, then add the armagnac or cognac and ignite it. Pour in the red wine and reduce it by half over high heat, then add the vegetable stock, juniper berries, thyme and bay leaf. Cook briskly to reduce the liquid by half, add the cream and bubble for another 3 minutes. Pass the sauce through a wire-mesh conical sieve, season with salt and pepper and serve immediately with the reserved breast and thigh meat.

Cranberry and Bilberry Sauce

I serve this sauce with terrines of game or pâtés en croûte. It is also good served just warm with wild roast goose. The berries, particularly bilberries, can sometimes be rather tart; if so, add about 30 g caster sugar to the sauce halfway through cooking.

Ingredients:

150 g cranberries
75 g caster sugar
1 clove, crushed
150 g bilberries
200 ml cold water
Juice of 1 lemon
Zest of the lemon, cut into julienne
and blanched

Serves 8

Preparation time: **5 minutes**

Cooking time: **about 30 minutes**

Put the cranberries in a saucepan, add 100 ml cold water, then the sugar and clove and cook gently for 10 minutes. Add the bilberries, the remaining cold water and the lemon juice and simmer for 20 minutes. Keep the sauce at room temperature; it should not be served too cold. If you prefer a very smooth sauce with no fruit skins, pass it through a strainer. Stir in the lemon zest just before serving.

Index

Index

Acknowledgements

This edition published in 2000 by
Quadrille Publishing Ltd
Alhambra House
27 – 31 Charing Cross Road
London WC2H 0LS

Based on material originally published
in *Sauces; sweet and savoury, classic
and new* by Michel Roux.

Text © 1996 & 2000 Michel Roux
Photography © 1996 Martin Brigdale
Design & layout © 2000
Quadrille Publishing Ltd

Publishing Director: **Anne Furniss**
Art Director: **Mary Evans**
Art Editor: **Rachel Gibson**
Project Editor & Translator: **Kate Whiteman**
Editorial Assistant: **Caroline Perkins**
Styling: **Helen Trent**
Production: **Rachel Wells**

All rights reserved. No part of this book may
be reproduced, stored in a retrieval system or
transmitted in any form or by any means,
electronic, electrostatic, magnetic tape,
mechanical, photocopying, recording or otherwise,
without the permission in writing of the publisher.

The right of Michel Roux to be identified as
the Author of this Work has been asserted by
him in accordance with the Copyright,
Designs and Patents Act 1988.

Cataloguing-in-Publication Date: a catalogue
record for this book is available from the
British Library.

ISBN 1 902757 39 4

Printed & bound by Dai Nippon Printing
Company Ltd, Hong Kong